THE PHILLIP KEVEREN SERIES — EASY PIANO DUETS

CLASSICAL THEME DUETS

CONTENTS

— PIANO LEVEL —
EARLY INTERMEDIATE

ISBN-13: 978-1-4234-1792-7

HAL•LEONARD®
CORPORATION
7777 W. BLUEMOUND RD. P.O. BOX 13819 MILWAUKEE, WI 53213

In Australia Contact:
Hal Leonard Australia Pty. Ltd.
22 Taunton Drive   P.O. Box 5130
Cheltenham East, 3192   Victoria, Australia
Email: ausadmin@halleonard.com

Visit Hal Leonard Online at
www.halleonard.com

Visit Phillip at
www.phillipkeveren.com

PREFACE

This collection features some of the most famous and intriguing classical themes from the worlds of orchestral music and opera. The piano duet format is an excellent way to explore this music without convening an entire orchestra! It would be very helpful to study an orchestral recording prior to learning one of these arrangements. That listening experience will be priceless as you interpret these settings at the piano.

I have fond memories of duet playing from my student days. I loved getting together with a friend and making music. So much can be learned from this collaborative experience... and it's a lot of fun!

With warm regards,
Phillip Keveren

BIOGRAPHY

Phillip Keveren, a multi-talented keyboard artist and composer, has composed original works in a variety of genres from piano solo to symphonic orchestra. Mr. Keveren gives frequent concerts and workshops for teachers and their students in the United States, Canada, Europe, and Asia. Mr. Keveren holds a B.M. in composition from California State University Northridge and a M.M. in composition from the University of Southern California.

SYMPHONY NO. 5 IN C MINOR
First Movement Excerpt

By LUDWIG VAN BEETHOVEN
Arranged by Phillip Keveren

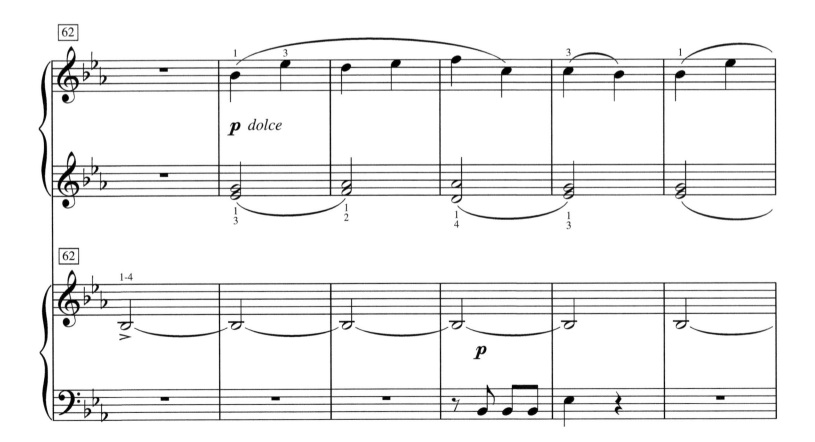

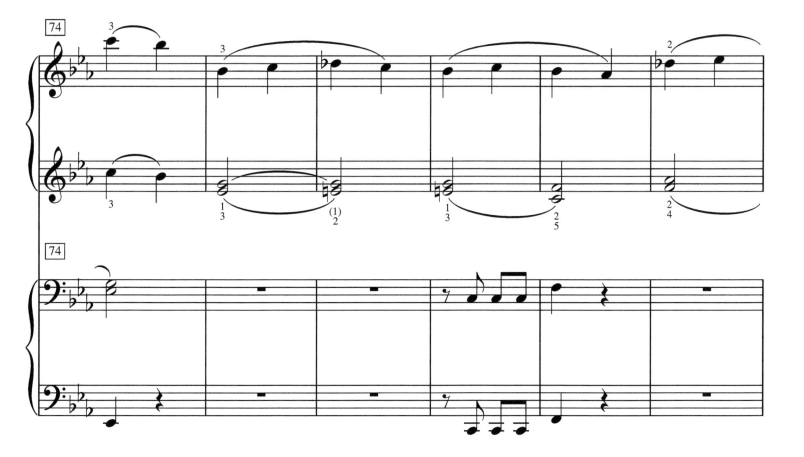

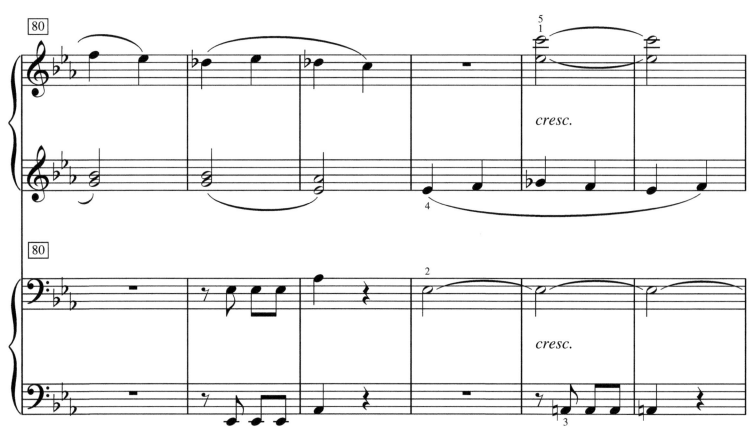

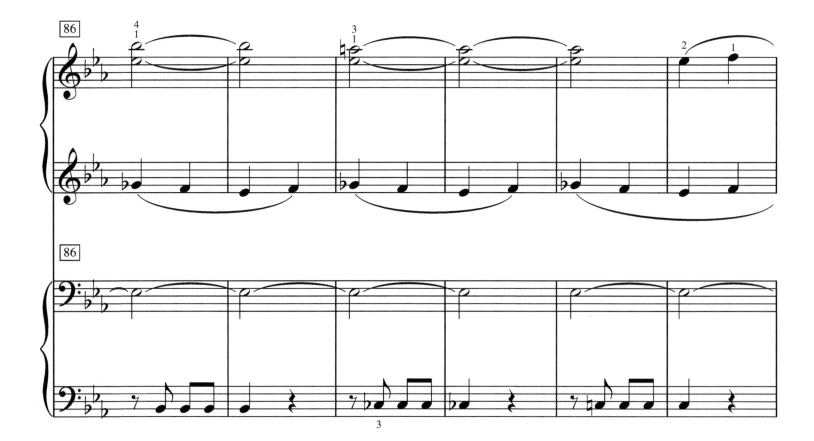

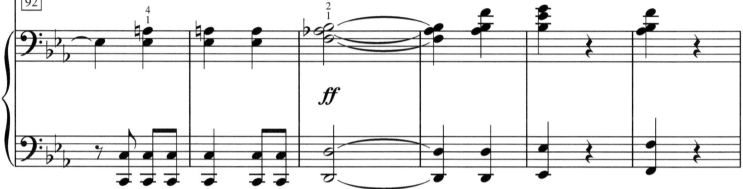

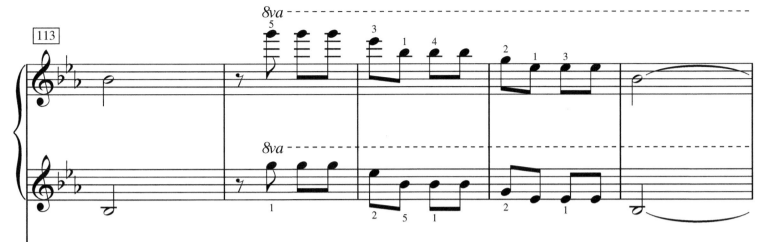

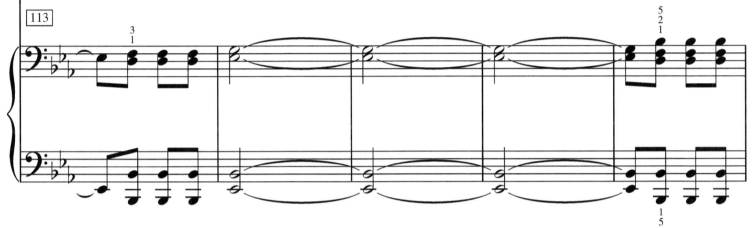

HABANERA
from CARMEN

By GEORGES BIZET
Arranged by Phillip Keveren

POLOVETSIAN DANCE
from PRINCE IGOR

By ALEXANDER BORODIN
Arranged by Phillip Keveren

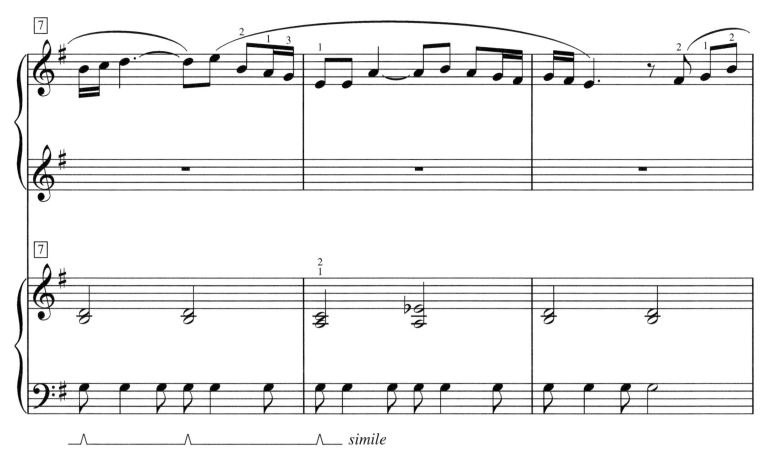

simile

FUNERAL MARCH OF A MARIONETTE

By CHARLES GOUNOD
Arranged by Phillip Keveren

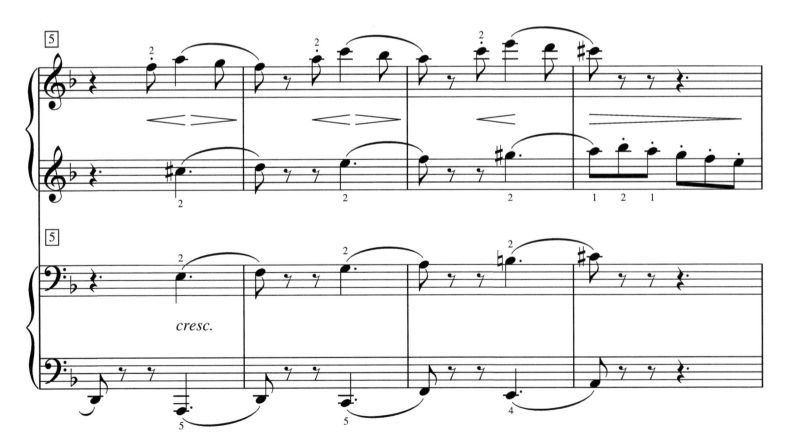

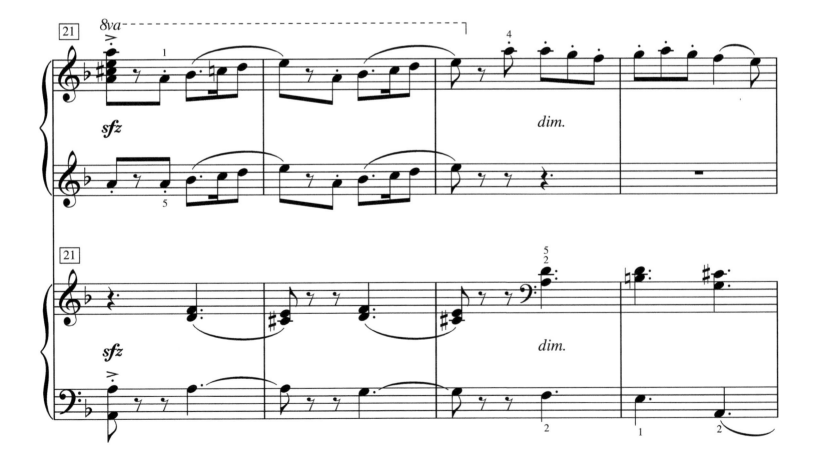

IN THE HALL OF THE MOUNTAIN KING

from PEER GYNT

By EDVARD GRIEG
Arranged by Phillip Keveren

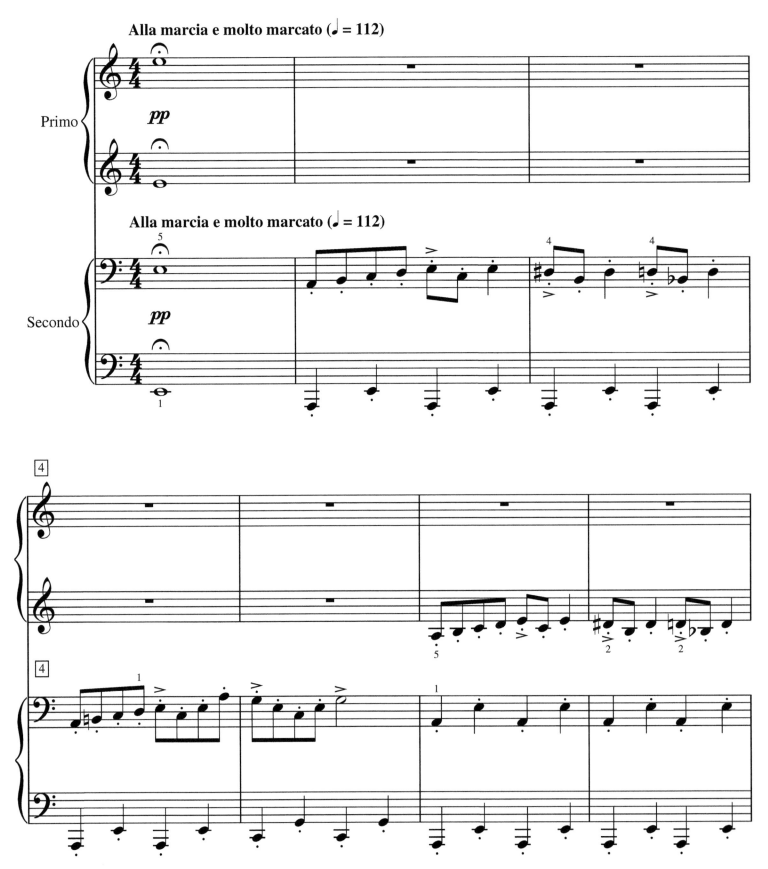

cresc. e accel. poco a poco

SYMPHONY NO. 40 IN G MINOR

First Movement Excerpt

By WOLFGANG AMADEUS MOZART
Arranged by Phillip Keveren

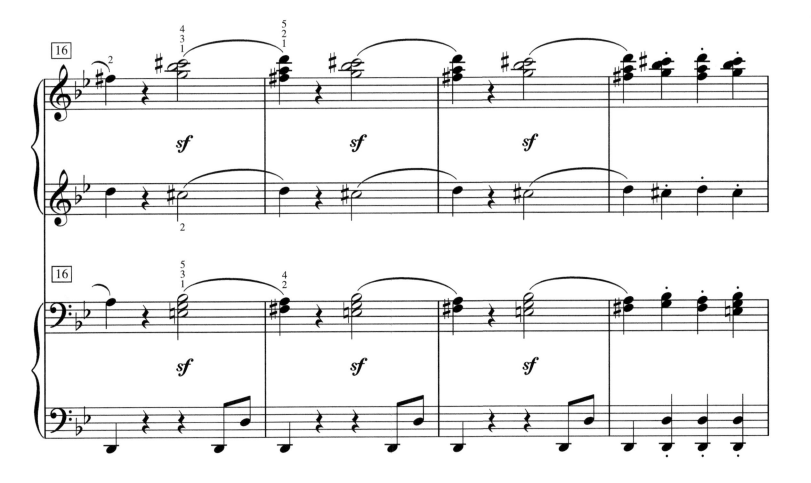

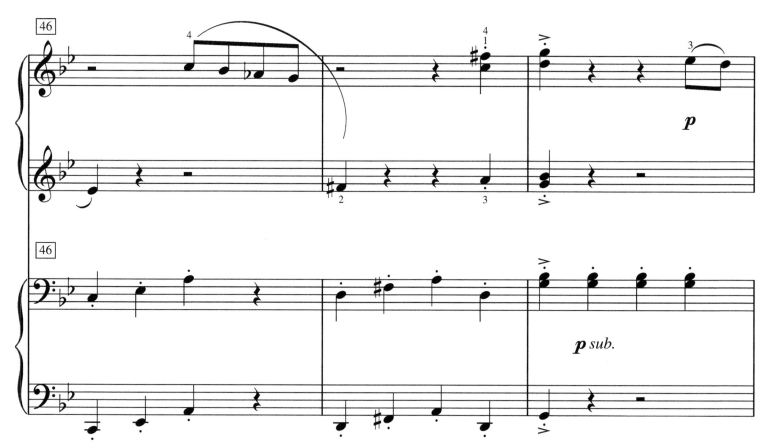

RUSSIAN DANCE
(Trépak)
from THE NUTCRACKER

By PYOTR IL'YICH TCHAIKOVSKY
Arranged by Phillip Keveren

Tempo di Trépak, molto vivace (♩ = 138)
Both hands 8va throughout

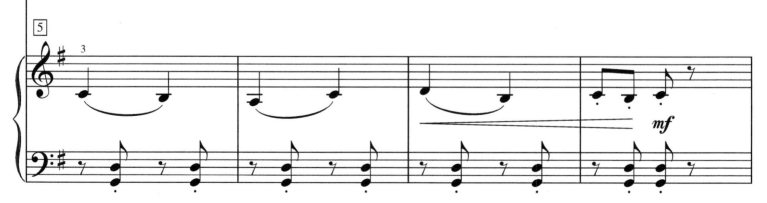

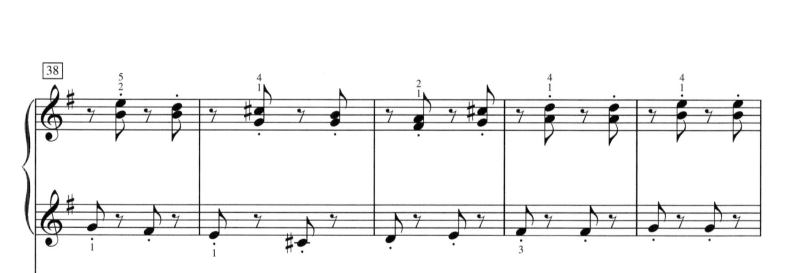

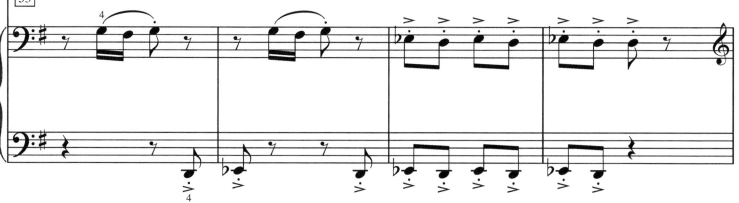

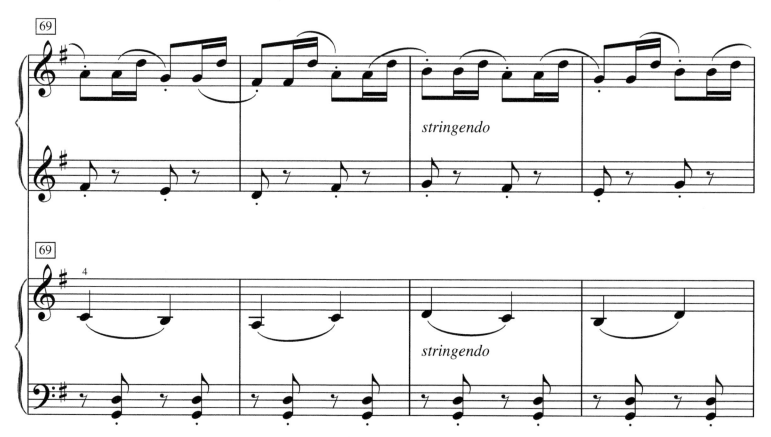

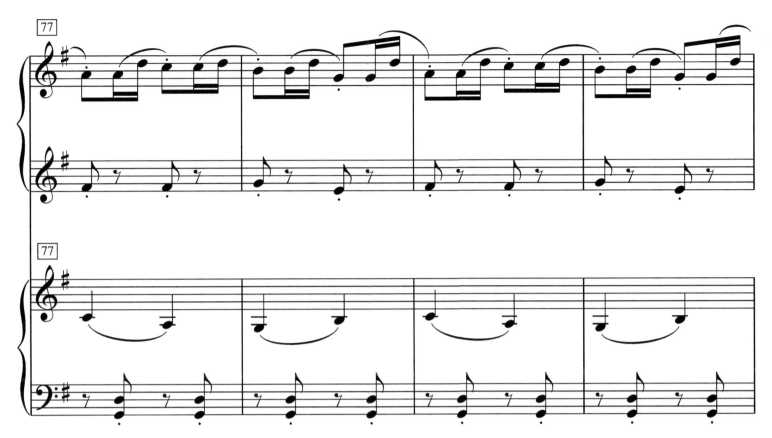

THE FOUR SEASONS
("Autumn")
First Movement Excerpt

By ANTONIO VIVALDI
Arranged by Phillip Keveren

THE PHILLIP KEVEREN SERIES

PIANO SOLO

00156644	**ABBA for Classical Piano**	$15.99
00311024	**Above All**	$12.99
00311348	**Americana**	$12.99
00198473	**Bach Meets Jazz**	$14.99
00313594	**Bacharach and David**	$15.99
00306412	**The Beatles**	$19.99
00312189	**The Beatles for Classical Piano**	$17.99
00275876	**The Beatles – Recital Suites**	$19.99
00312546	**Best Piano Solos**	$15.99
00156601	**Blessings**	$14.99
00198656	**Blues Classics**	$14.99
00284359	**Broadway Songs with a Classical Flair**	$14.99
00310669	**Broadway's Best**	$16.99
00312106	**Canzone Italiana**	$12.99
00280848	**Carpenters**	$17.99
00310629	**A Celtic Christmas**	$14.99
00310549	**The Celtic Collection**	$14.99
00280571	**Celtic Songs with a Classical Flair**	$12.99
00263362	**Charlie Brown Favorites**	$14.99
00312190	**Christmas at the Movies**	$15.99
00294754	**Christmas Carols with a Classical Flair**	$12.99
00311414	**Christmas Medleys**	$14.99
00236669	**Christmas Praise Hymns**	$12.99
00233788	**Christmas Songs for Classical Piano**	$14.99
00311769	**Christmas Worship Medleys**	$14.99
00310607	**Cinema Classics**	$15.99
00301857	**Circles**	$10.99
00311101	**Classic Wedding Songs**	$12.99
00311292	**Classical Folk**	$10.95
00311083	**Classical Jazz**	$14.99
00137779	**Coldplay for Classical Piano**	$16.99
00311103	**Contemporary Wedding Songs**	$12.99
00348788	**Country Songs with a Classical Flair**	$14.99
00249097	**Disney Recital Suites**	$17.99
00311754	**Disney Songs for Classical Piano**	$17.99
00241379	**Disney Songs for Ragtime Piano**	$17.99
00364812	**The Essential Hymn Anthology**	$34.99
00311881	**Favorite Wedding Songs**	$14.99
00315974	**Fiddlin' at the Piano**	$12.99
00311811	**The Film Score Collection**	$15.99
00269408	**Folksongs with a Classical Flair**	$12.99
00144353	**The Gershwin Collection**	$14.99
00233789	**Golden Scores**	$14.99
00144351	**Gospel Greats**	$14.99
00183566	**The Great American Songbook**	$14.99
00312084	**The Great Melodies**	$14.99
00311157	**Great Standards**	$14.99
00171621	**A Grown-Up Christmas List**	$14.99
00311071	**The Hymn Collection**	$14.99
00311349	**Hymn Medleys**	$14.99
00280705	**Hymns in a Celtic Style**	$14.99

00269407	**Hymns with a Classical Flair**	$14.99
00311249	**Hymns with a Touch of Jazz**	$14.99
00310905	**I Could Sing of Your Love Forever**	$16.99
00310762	**Jingle Jazz**	$15.99
00175310	**Billy Joel for Classical Piano**	$16.99
00126449	**Elton John for Classical Piano**	$19.99
00310839	**Let Freedom Ring!**	$12.99
00238988	**Andrew Lloyd Webber Piano Songbook**	$14.99
00313227	**Andrew Lloyd Webber Solos**	$17.99
00313523	**Mancini Magic**	$16.99
00312113	**More Disney Songs for Classical Piano**	$16.99
00311295	**Motown Hits**	$14.99
00300640	**Piano Calm**	$12.99
00339131	**Piano Calm: Christmas**	$14.99
00346009	**Piano Calm: Prayer**	$14.99
00306870	**Piazzolla Tangos**	$17.99
00386709	**Praise and Worship for Classical Piano**	$14.99
00156645	**Queen for Classical Piano**	$17.99
00310755	**Richard Rodgers Classics**	$17.99
00289545	**Scottish Songs**	$12.99
00119403	**The Sound of Music**	$16.99
00311978	**The Spirituals Collection**	$12.99
00366023	**So Far...**	$14.99
00210445	**Star Wars**	$16.99
00224738	**Symphonic Hymns for Piano**	$14.99
00366022	**Three-Minute Encores**	$16.99
00279673	**Tin Pan Alley**	$12.99
00312112	**Treasured Hymns for Classical Piano**	$15.99
00144926	**The Twelve Keys of Christmas**	$14.99
00278486	**The Who for Classical Piano**	$16.99
00294036	**Worship with a Touch of Jazz**	$14.99
00311911	**Yuletide Jazz**	$19.99

EASY PIANO

00210401	**Adele for Easy Classical Piano**	$17.99
00310610	**African-American Spirituals**	$12.99
00218244	**The Beatles for Easy Classical Piano**	$14.99
00218387	**Catchy Songs for Piano**	$12.99
00310973	**Celtic Dreams**	$12.99
00233686	**Christmas Carols for Easy Classical Piano**	$14.99
00311126	**Christmas Pops**	$16.99
00368199	**Christmas Reflections**	$14.99
00311548	**Classic Pop/Rock Hits**	$14.99
00310769	**A Classical Christmas**	$14.99
00310975	**Classical Movie Themes**	$12.99
00144352	**Disney Songs for Easy Classical Piano**	$14.99
00311093	**Early Rock 'n' Roll**	$14.99
00311997	**Easy Worship Medleys**	$14.99
00289547	**Duke Ellington**	$14.99
00160297	**Folksongs for Easy Classical Piano**	$12.99

00110374	**George Gershwin Classics**	$14.99
00310805	**Gospel Treasures**	$14.99
00306821	**Vince Guaraldi Collection**	$19.99
00160294	**Hymns for Easy Classical Piano**	$14.99
00310798	**Immortal Hymns**	$12.99
00311294	**Jazz Standards**	$12.99
00355474	**Living Hope**	$14.99
00310744	**Love Songs**	$14.99
00233740	**The Most Beautiful Songs for Easy Classical Piano**	$12.99
00220036	**Pop Ballads**	$14.99
00311406	**Pop Gems of the 1950s**	$12.95
00233739	**Pop Standards for Easy Classical Piano**	$12.99
00102887	**A Ragtime Christmas**	$12.99
00311293	**Ragtime Classics**	$14.99
00312028	**Santa Swings**	$14.99
00233688	**Songs from Childhood for Easy Classical Piano**	$12.99
00103258	**Songs of Inspiration**	$14.99
00310840	**Sweet Land of Liberty**	$12.99
00126450	**10,000 Reasons**	$16.99
00310712	**Timeless Praise**	$14.99
00311086	**TV Themes**	$14.99
00310717	**21 Great Classics**	$14.99
00160076	**Waltzes & Polkas for Easy Classical Piano**	$12.99
00145342	**Weekly Worship**	$17.99

BIG-NOTE PIANO

00310838	**Children's Favorite Movie Songs**	$14.99
00346000	**Christmas Movie Magic**	$12.99
00277368	**Classical Favorites**	$12.99
00277370	**Disney Favorites**	$14.99
00310888	**Joy to the World**	$12.99
00310908	**The Nutcracker**	$12.99
00277371	**Star Wars**	$16.99

BEGINNING PIANO SOLOS

00311202	**Awesome God**	$14.99
00310837	**Christian Children's Favorites**	$14.99
00311117	**Christmas Traditions**	$10.99
00311250	**Easy Hymns**	$12.99
00102710	**Everlasting God**	$10.99
00311403	**Jazzy Tunes**	$10.95
00310822	**Kids' Favorites**	$12.99
00367778	**A Magical Christmas**	$14.99
00338175	**Silly Songs for Kids**	$9.99

PIANO DUET

00126452	**The Christmas Variations**	$14.99
00362562	**Classic Piano Duets**	$14.99
00311350	**Classical Theme Duets**	$12.99
00295099	**Gospel Duets**	$12.99
00311544	**Hymn Duets**	$14.99
00311203	**Praise & Worship Duets**	$14.99
00294755	**Sacred Christmas Duets**	$14.99
00119405	**Star Wars**	$16.99
00253545	**Worship Songs for Two**	$12.99

Prices, contents, and availability subject to change without notice.

HAL•LEONARD®

Search songlists, more products and place your order from your favorite music retailer at **halleonard.com**

Disney characters and artwork
TM & © 2021 Disney LLC